# ROUGH & READY
# PROSPECTORS

A. S. GINTZLER

FITZGERALD
BOOKS
BETHANY, MISSOURI

# Acknowledgments

To the prospectors and their chroniclers.

First Hardcover Library Bound Edition
Published in 1998 by Fitzgerald Books
P.O. Box 505, Bethany, Missouri 64424

Library of Congress Cataloging-in-Publication Data
Gintzler, A. S.
Rough and ready prospectors / A. S. Gintzler
   p.   cm.
   Includes index.
ISBN 1-887238-11-5
1. Gold mines and mining—West (U.S.)—History—19th century—Juvenile literature. 2. Gold miners—West (U.S.)—History—Juvenile literature. [1. Gold mines and mining. 2. California—Gold discoveries.] I. Title.
TN423.A5G55 1998
622'.3422'0978—dc20

97-78365
CIP
AC

Logo & Cover Design: Paul Perlow
Interior Design and Typography: Linda Braun
Illustrations: Chris Brigman
Printer: Burton & Mayer, Inc.
Title page photo, Miners weighing their gold
   dust, ca. 1900 © UPI/Bettmann

*Miners using a sluice box to find gold*

# CONTENTS

Gold in the Americas ...................................................... 2

"Gold Fever" ................................................................... 4

Routes to the Gold ......................................................... 6

The Gold Seekers ........................................................... 8

Life in the Diggings ..................................................... 10

The Geology of Gold ................................................... 12

The Prospector's Tools ................................................ 14

Hard-Rock Mining ....................................................... 16

Dangers of Mining ...................................................... 18

Gold and Silver Rushes ............................................... 20

Mining Towns .............................................................. 22

Law and Disorder ........................................................ 24

Indians on the Mining Frontier ................................... 26

Mule Trains and Muleteers .......................................... 28

Songs of the Forty-Niners ........................................... 30

In the Miners' Own Words .......................................... 32

Tall Tales of the Gold Rush ........................................ 34

Bonanza Kings and Paupers ........................................ 36

Ghost Towns ................................................................ 38

Mining and the Environment ....................................... 40

Prospecting Today ....................................................... 42

Index ............................................................................ 45

The Bettmann Archive

# Gold in the Americas

*Aztec goldsmiths*

Pure gold is a soft, shiny, sun-yellow metal, easy to bend and shape. People have been wild about gold throughout history. As early as 15,000 B.C., prehistoric people pounded the bright metal into ornaments. In ancient China, small gold cubes were used as money. West African kings stored glittery gold dust in hollow quills.

Ancient peoples on the South American continent prized gold, too. Mexico's Aztecs and the Incas of Peru crafted gold ornaments. Spanish explorers traveled to the New World looking for such riches. When the Spaniards conquered the Incas in 1533, they stole their gold jewelry, plates, and other golden objects and shipped them back to Spain.

The Spanish explorer Coronado heard stories of "golden cities" to the north. He marched his army into what is now Arizona and New Mexico in 1540 to find them. Instead, he found only Indian towns built of stone and mud. He returned to Mexico empty-handed.

*Striking gold*

Spanish missionaries were the first Europeans to settle California, now known as the "Golden State." They claimed the land for themselves, built ranches, and tried to convert Native Americans to Catholicism. In 1821, Mexico gained its independence from Spain and claimed California as its own. Mexicans began moving into the territory, and some of them began digging for gold.

On a ranch belonging to Juan Manuel Vaca, Mexicans mined about a dollar's worth of gold a day. The Mexican governor of California wanted to develop more mines, but the Mexican government didn't want to spend money on California mining. Mexican officials didn't think there was enough gold in California to make it worthwhile. They were dead wrong.

The Bettmann Archive

From 1846 to 1848, the United States fought a war with Mexico over ownership of California and the area that is now Arizona and New Mexico. This conflict became known as the Mexican-American War. The United States won the war and claimed the lands—just in time for the Gold Rush.

On January 24, 1848, a carpenter named John Marshall found gold while building a sawmill on the American River in northern California. The mill was owned by a landowner named John Sutter. Marshall spotted a dime-sized yellow nugget in a water ditch at the mill and called out to his crew, "Boys, I believe I have found a gold mine!" They thought he was kidding.

Marshall brought the gold to Sutter. Together they decided to keep it a secret, but the news leaked out. In May, a man named Sam Brannan visited the diggings at Sutter's mill. He returned to San Francisco and ran through the streets with a bottle of gold flakes, shouting, "Gold! Gold! Gold on the American River!"

*A San Francisco café during Gold Rush days*

Stories appeared in the San Francisco newspapers about the gold strike at Sutter's mill. Within days, Californians flocked to the Sacramento area to find their own gold. "Gold fever" swept like wildfire across the nation and around the world. There was no stopping the stampede of gold seekers once they heard there was "gold in them thar' hills!"

## AN EARLY RUSH

The gold strike at Sutter's mill in 1848 wasn't the first in California. In 1842, Francisco Lopez struck gold in San Feliciano Canyon. Miners there didn't have enough water for washing gravels, however, so the gold yield was low. In 1843, a California landowner named Abel Stearns sent 20 ounces of this gold to the Philadelphia mint. It was the first shipment of California gold back East.

# "Gold Fever"

News of Marshall's discovery of gold at Sutter's mill traveled fast. By June of 1848, almost all of San Francisco's 800 citizens had left for the Sierra foothills in search of gold. Sailors left their ships anchored in San Francisco harbor and headed for the hills. They dreamed of striking it rich. They had caught "gold fever."

There were no radios or telephones then, but news spread by boat to Hawaii and China and up the west coast to Oregon. Gold fever swept down into Mexico and Chile and eventually reached east to New York. The governor of California wrote a report to President Polk saying that nuggets weighing up to 25 pounds had been found. In December of 1848, President Polk reported the news in his annual speech to Congress. The Gold Rush was on.

*"Gold fever" spread across the country like wildfire*

Even before the president's speech, 5,000 gold seekers were already panning for gold in the Sierra Nevada foothills. By the end of 1849, 40,000 people were digging for gold in California. And many more were on the way. The people who rushed to California in 1849 became known as "forty-niners." That's why, today, San Francisco's football team calls itself the "49ers."

The day after President Polk's speech, a ship left Boston with gold seekers bound for San Francisco. They had to sail all the way around the tip of South America to get there. By February, a total of 136 ships had left the East Coast for the gold fields. "Gold" was the word on everyone's lips. Barbers, bartenders, sailors, preachers—everyone talked about it. Newspapers and magazines stirred people's dreams with ads for tickets to the West.

Guidebooks promising to lead the way to gold were sold to hopeful gold seekers. But many of these guides were written by people who had never even been to California. So-called "facts" were based on rumors. Most North Americans arrived at the gold fields knowing nothing about mining gold. The experienced miners came from Mexico, Chile, Ireland, and England.

News of the gold strike traveled to Europe, China, Australia, and South America. Before 1848, there were only 14,000 non-Indians living in California. By 1852, the non-Indian population had grown to 224,000. And more than 25,000 Chinese had arrived in California to mine by 1855.

Most of the gold seekers were young single men. Few families and few women and children joined the rush. The men hoped to strike gold, get rich quick, and return home. Some who joined

*Hopeful prospectors heading for California*

the rush didn't plan to dig for gold at all. They were merchants and businessmen who hoped to get rich by selling goods to miners. Many did.

The California Gold Rush was only the first of several gold rushes. By the 1850s, prospectors were moving north and west to newer gold frontiers. Ten years after the forty-niners flooded California, "fifty-niners" headed to Nevada and Colorado after hearing news of other gold strikes. Later gold rushes drew miners to Montana, Idaho, the Black Hills of South Dakota, and Alaska.

## WOMEN FORTY-NINERS

By the end of 1848, one Oregon newspaper reported that "almost the entire male population had gone gold digging in California." But a few women caught gold fever, too. Though it was considered "unladylike," these courageous women headed west to find husbands, mine gold, and start businesses. One shrewd businesswoman, Luzena Wilson, cooked for hundreds of miners in Nevada City, California. She also became their banker—storing their gold dust in milk pails and under her mattress.

*Some women started businesses in the mining camps*

5

# Routes to the Gold

The forty-niner's first task was getting to California. Traveling by land from the Missouri frontier took four to five months. The sea route around the tip of South America took six months. And the combined sea and land route through Panama took five or more weeks. All of these routes were dangerous. Many people died along the way.

Before the rush to California began, ocean steamships carried mail from New York to Panama. Wagons then took the mail to the Pacific coast, where it was put on another ship to California.

In January of 1848, a mail ship called the *California* was mobbed by gold seekers in Panama who wanted to get to California. Four hundred people crowded on board the ship, which was built to hold only 100. When the *California* reached San Francisco, even the crew jumped ship for the gold fields. San Francisco's ports were soon jammed with empty ships, abandoned by gold-hungry sailors.

The Panama route was the quickest, but it was often deadly. In Panama's dense jungles, many people became ill with malaria, cholera, or yellow fever, and died along the way. By

The Bettmann Archive

*Gold seekers trekking through the jungles of Panama*

1855, transportation through Panama's jungles was improved by 47 miles of railroad. But dangers still existed. In 1853, the steamship *San Francisco* wrecked in a storm. Two hundred passengers were killed. Still, most of the early forty-niners arrived in San Francisco by way of Panama.

Others from the East chose to avoid the Panama route. Gold seekers formed themselves into small companies and rented sailing ships. They sailed 17,000 sea miles around Cape Horn, the tip of South America, to San Francisco. In 1849, a total of 775 ships sailed from eastern ports for California.

Overland travelers had to cross the western deserts. Water was scarce. Horse and mule teams went without food since there was no grass to be found. Many animals died in their tracks. Wagons and supplies were abandoned. The Carson route wound through 45 miles of desert sands. One traveler counted 3,000 head of dead livestock and 700 abandoned wagons along the route. No wonder the last ten miles of the route were called Destruction Valley.

*Many died crossing the hot desert*

During the six months at sea, passengers entertained themselves with card games, plays, lectures, fishing, and sporting contests. The sea route was long, but safer than the Panama route. Most gold seekers who sailed around the "Horn" arrived safely.

The most-traveled route was by land. This route began at the edge of the western frontier in Missouri. The only way west for frontier farmers and townspeople was over the Oregon and Santa Fe Trails from Independence, Missouri. These trails crossed through 2,000 miles of rough wilderness. Gold seekers banded together in small groups and loaded covered wagons for the crossing. They harnessed teams of mules, horses, or oxen to pull their heavy loads.

But the trails were full of dangers. The greatest hazard was disease. The overland trails were marked with the fresh graves of cholera victims. Many horses and cattle died crossing the desert. Wagons broke down and supplies had to be abandoned. Wagons and trunks were broken apart and burned as firewood.

Despite these dangers, some 55,000 gold seekers took the overland routes in 1850 alone. Those who survived the journey were worn out, if not sick, by the time they reached California. But the strongest quickly headed for the gold fields.

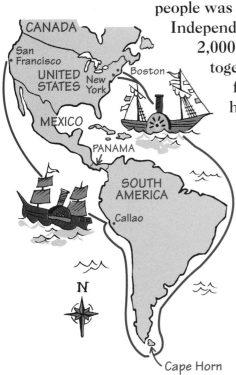

*The sea route around Cape Horn*

# The Gold Seekers

**A**long beard and dusty hair, floppy hat and muddy boots—this is the popular image of the old-time prospector. But it really isn't very accurate. Not all miners looked alike, talked alike, and played "Oh, Susanna" on a banjo or fiddle. The gold rushes attracted gold seekers of all sorts. Farmers from Missouri and Oregon, lawyers from New York, and sailors from Boston all joined in the search for gold. One East Coast company that came west included two clergymen, four doctors, eight whaling captains, and 76 mechanics. None had ever prospected before.

The Chileans, Mexicans, Irish, and British who came, however, brought mining skills with them. Sonorans from northern Mexico borrowed their "grubstake"—money and provisions—from wealthy landowners. They camped with their wives and children in the Sierra foothills. The town they settled came to be called Sonora, after their home in Mexico.

Hawaiians, Chinese, and Australians also came. But they, like most gold seekers, didn't bring their wives and children. In fact, in 1850 over 90 percent of the non-Indian population of California was male. These men didn't plan to settle for good. Their hope was to strike it rich and return to their families back home. Many did return—most of them with empty pockets.

*An old-timer with his trusty mule*

Denver Public Library

## CHINESE MINERS

About 600 Chinese were panning for California gold in 1850. Just two years later, there were 25,000 hopeful Chinese miners. But unlike the Irish, Welsh, and German miners, the Chinese weren't accepted by the Americans. They were segregated and forced out of the best gold areas. Still, by 1860 about 285,000 Chinese miners worked in California's Sierra foothills.

*A Chinese miner using a rocker*

The Bettmann Archive

Before the strike at Sutter's mill in 1848, about 14,000 non-Indians were living in California. Just one year later, the population had jumped to 100,000. Not all of these people were miners. Many were businessmen, shopkeepers, bankers, and carpenters. About 5,000 men actually worked the mines in 1848. One year later, 40,000 men were mining in California.

*Gold seekers came to California from all over the world*

In the deep mines of Nevada's Comstock Lode, most of the workers were from other countries. In 1880, nearly three-quarters of the 2,770 Comstock miners were foreign-born. Almost half of these Sierra silver miners brought mining experience with them from England. In California, the Mexicans who came shared their knowledge of mining.

The Bettmann Archive

*A prospector poses with his tools, around 1860*

In the early days of the California Gold Rush, there wasn't much difference between prospectors and miners. A prospector staked a claim and mined it himself or with a small group of partners. After most of the loose gold in streams was gathered, however, prospectors had to begin digging into rocky hillsides to find more gold. This was called "hard-rock" mining, and it took teams of men and equipment.

Lone hard-rock prospectors dug into the hills to find signs of gold. After finding it, they usually sold their claim to the men who operated the mines. The operators then hired teams of miners to do the hard work of tunneling into the mountainside and freeing the gold from the surrounding stone.

As late as the 1870s and 1880s, a few solitary prospectors still roamed the Sierras and Rockies. Meanwhile, hard-rock miners worked for big mining companies, blasting deep underground tunnels for a daily wage.

# Life in the Diggings

**W**hen a prospector arrived at a mining camp, he pitched his tent and started digging. California's gold camps, known as the "diggings," were scattered throughout the Sierra Nevada mountains. Camps with names like Poverty Bar, You Bet, Poker Flat, and Fiddletown sprung up wherever prospectors struck gold. Similar camps popped up in the Rocky Mountains.

Mining camps were born when a prospector struck a claim and others followed. Some camps—like the ones in Central City, Colorado,

*An early mining camp*

or Butte, Montana—became "boom" towns. They exploded into large business centers. But most mining camps were tiny settlements with just a few rickety buildings. Prospectors settled and mined these isolated areas for as long as the gold held out. Then they packed up their bedrolls, shouldered their pickaxes, and moved on.

Miners weren't interested in building homes and putting down roots. They came for gold and planned to leave when the deposits gave out. Most expected to return to their families and friends back home in Missouri, Mexico, China, or elsewhere. So they built flimsy shacks and tent dwellings, or dug caves out of mountainsides.

They picked and washed gravel six days a week, let their hair and beards grow, and ate poor food. Unclean living conditions brought disease and insects like fleas, lice, and mites. Prospectors removed lice from their clothing daily.

*Washday at the diggings*

## THE GENERAL STORE

Miners crowding into a new camp needed supplies, so all mining towns had a general store. They stocked everything from groceries and clothes to pickaxes, medicines, and liquor. General stores usually had two rooms. Goods were displayed in the front room, while the merchant lived in the back room. General stores also served as post offices and banks. Miners often paid for their supplies in gold.

Sunday was washday. A miner pounded and scrubbed his dirty trousers and red flannel shirt, then hung them up to dry. He had only one change of clothes. He cooked over an open fire, baking flat cakes in a skillet or fresh bread in a portable oven. He ate salt pork, beef jerky, and even bacon that had gone bad—anything to fill his growling stomach.

From the start, miners organized their own town governments. They also made their own entertainment. Card playing for pinches of gold was very popular. Miners also whittled wood or made their own music to amuse themselves after work. At the diggings, they put on dances. Since women were scarce, miners danced with each other. Other popular entertainments were bull-and-bear fights, cock fights, and bear-and-jackass battles.

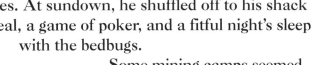
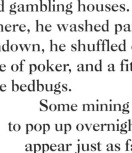

*Prospectors kick up their heels at a "miners' ball"*

From time to time, prospectors traveled to the larger boom towns like San Francisco, Sacramento, or Virginia City. In the cities they found saloons, dance halls, and gambling houses. But the prospector's life was centered at the diggings. There, he washed pan after pan of gravel with an eye peeled for gold flakes. At sundown, he shuffled off to his shack for a meal, a game of poker, and a fitful night's sleep with the bedbugs.

Some mining camps seemed to pop up overnight—only to disappear just as fast. Prospectors built rows of shacks or simple wooden frames covered with canvas. Narrow dirt streets filled up with saloons and supply shops. Silver Reef, Utah boomed to a town of over a thousand during the 1880s. But by 1890, only 177 people remained. Life in the diggings came and went in a flash.

*Miners lived in tents and rickety shacks*

# The Geology of Gold

**G**old is found all over the Earth, in land and sea. But how did it get there? The answer lies buried in our planet's geology, or physical history.

Geologists tell us that the Earth was once a mass of hot melted rock. As it cooled, the Earth formed different layers. We live on the hard outer layer, called the "crust." Under the crust is a layer that is still partly melted, called the "outer mantle." Melted rock in this outer mantle is called magma and contains many minerals, such as gold, silver, and quartz.

As the Earth cooled, its crust heaved and cracked. This melted rock—some of it containing gold, silver, and other minerals— seeped up through these cracks and hardened. That's why gold is found in certain "veins" of rock, also called "lodes." Some veins are pure gold, but most gold was left mixed together with quartz and other rock.

*Veins of Gold and Silver*

*Magma*

*Magma seeps into cracks in the crust, depositing minerals such as gold*

As the planet aged, volcanoes erupted and the Earth's crust wrinkled, forming the giant mountain ranges that we have today. Rains, winds, and storms eroded the land. Great oceans came and went, covering land that today is dry desert. Ancient rivers carved mountain valleys, then changed their course or dried up completely. Parts of the Earth's crust collided with other parts, causing powerful earthquakes. All of these upheavals exposed and broke apart the rock that holds gold deposits.

*Mountain Stream Carrying Gold Grains*

*Gold Veins*

*Gold Flakes Settle in Stream Bed*

*Gold flows from mountaintops to valley stream beds*

## THE FLOW OF GOLD

At first, all gold is trapped inside hard rock. Over millions of years, earthquakes and erosion expose the rock and break it into pieces. The pieces tumble downhill and get stuck behind boulders. Rain and wind pound the rock and break it into even smaller pieces or flakes. These flakes of loose gold are washed downhill into streams, where they sink into stream beds. And there they sit, waiting for a prospector.

*The Bettmann Archive*

*Panning for gold*

For millions of years rivers formed and cut through the mountains, tearing gold from old veins. Chunks of rock washed downstream and broke into gravel. Erosion wore gravel into sand. The sand and gravel were swept down mountainsides to stream beds below. Wherever water flowed, it carried bits of gold mixed with gravel and sand.

Gold is very dense, or heavy—much heavier than sand or gravel. As gold-bearing rocks were ground apart by the water in streams, flakes and nuggets of heavy gold sank into cracks in stream beds. Other bits of gold were deposited in gravel bars at curves and bends in the stream. Gold-bearing rocks were trapped by roots, boulders, and cracks in the stream bed. These gold deposits are called "placer" deposits.

Forty-niners first found gold in these placer deposits. Later, they prospected farther upstream to find the gold source. They located veins of gold in the hard rock of the mountainside. Mining gold from this hard rock is called hard-rock mining, quartz mining, or lode mining.

*The Bettmann Archive*

*Bars of gold*

# The Prospector's Tools

California's early gold seekers worked placer deposits along streams in the Sierra foothills. After finding a placer deposit, the forty-niner's task was to separate the gold from the gravel and sand in streams. To do this, he used a method called "panning" for gold.

A gold pan is about three inches deep, with sloping sides and a flat bottom. First, the prospector scooped up a pan of gravel and water. Then he removed the larger rocks and slowly swirled the mixture of pebbles, sand, and gravel.

Because gold is heavier than rock, any gold in the mixture would work its way to the bottom of the pan. Meanwhile the lighter sands and gravels slid out over the edge of the pan with the swirling water. If the mixture yielded gold, it was called "pay dirt."

After about ten minutes of panning, only the heavier bits of gold and black sand remained in the pan.

Placer miners knelt in ice-cold streams, washing fifty pans a day. But a day's work of panning usually yielded only an ounce of gold. Miners needed better ways to wash greater amounts of pay dirt.

The Bettmann Archive

*Prospectors panning at Rockerville, Dakota*

## COYOTING

"Coyotes" were holes and tunnels dug through gravel to bedrock, which is the solid rock that lies underneath soil and loose pieces of rock. Coyote holes were usually very narrow, with just enough room for one man to squirm through. As the hole deepened, side tunnels were dug to the main hole. Miners removed the gold-bearing gravels in buckets and carted them by wheelbarrow to a stream for washing. Coyoting was useful, but dangerous. When coyote tunnels caved in, many miners were smothered or crushed to death.

The Bettmann Archive

*Lowering a bucket into a coyote hole*

A more effective tool was the "rocker," also called the "cradle." A rocker was a large wooden box open at one end with curved rockers on the bottom. Nailed to the bottom of the open end was a strip of wood to catch and hold in the heaviest gravel.

*Placer miners used shovels, pans, and pickaxes*

Prospectors poured dirt into the box through a screen to sift out large rocks. Then they poured water in with the gravel and rocked the box very hard. The wooden strip at the bottom of the open side caught the heavy gold-bearing rock while the other gravel was washed out. Placer miners could wash three times more pay dirt in a day with their rockers than they could with pans.

Another tool called the "tom," or "long tom," was similar to the rocker. Where the rocker had a single piece of wood to catch the gold, the tom had a long wooden trough with strips of wood nailed across the bottom of it. As the water and gravel washed over the wooden strips, the heavy gold flakes were trapped behind them. Prospectors could wash five times more pay dirt in a day with a tom than with a pan.

To trap even more gold, miners attached several toms end to end to form a "sluice," or "sluice box." Sluice boxes were sometimes placed in the stream itself to use water currents for washing gravels.

Forty-niners also dug ditches and built dams to drain water from stream beds. This was called river mining and allowed miners to get at the gravel along the river bottoms. From pan to sluice to river mining, the forty-niner's tools and methods applied to placer deposits. Hard-rock mining came later. It took more money and planning.

*Miners using a long tom*

# Hard-Rock Mining

At first, the forty-niners worked only placer deposits in the Sierra Nevada foothills. Gradually, however, they worked their way up the mountain slopes toward the source of the gold. They found deposits of gold in veins that ran deep into solid bedrock.

Using pickaxes, the miners removed chunks of a gold-bearing rock called quartz. When this quartz was crushed into small pieces, much of the gold trapped inside was freed. This was the beginning of hard-rock mining, also called quartz mining.

*Using picks and hammers to chip away at solid rock*

Most placer mining was done by individuals, although small groups of prospectors sometimes banded together to build sluices, ditches, and flumes (channels to hold running water). But hard-rock mining took more machinery, more technical know-how, and more miners. Hard-rock miners had to find and trace veins, tunnel through solid rock, and remove heavy rubble. Then they had to crush the quartz and separate out the gold.

Early hard-rock mines were small, with shallow tunnels. But huge amounts of gold were freed from quartz veins. After the gold close to the surface was mined, the tunnels were made longer and deeper.

Mining companies were formed to fund these costly operations. Businessmen from back East and from Europe became owners of quartz mines in the Far West. And many old-time prospectors became hard-rock miners, working for a monthly paycheck.

*An arrastra, a type of Mexican mill*

To free trapped gold, the quartz had to be crushed. New machinery was needed. South American and Mexican miners had used a mill called an arrastra to crush stone.

Arrastras crushed quartz by dragging a heavy stone across the top of smaller quartz rocks. The stone was attached with a rope to a long wooden pole that was anchored at one end so it would rotate in a circle. The pole was harnessed to a mule. As the mule walked in a circle, the mill stones turned and crushed the quartz.

Another mill called a stamp mill used huge iron hammers to "stamp," or pound, on the quartz. The hammers were lifted by gears powered by steam engines. They were then dropped to crash down on the quartz. The "California stamp" traveled with quartz miners to Nevada. Between 1859 and 1880 quartz mining grew to be a big industry at Nevada's Comstock mines.

*Underground tunnels were supported by wooden beams*

Miners there tunneled through thousands of feet of hard rock. They supported the ceilings and walls of the tunnels with wood beams to prevent cave-ins. They dug air shafts for ventilation and removed underground water with pumps. They used drills invented in France and dynamite from Sweden.

To separate Comstock's gold and silver from the crushed rock, other new technologies were created. Placer miners in California had used mercury to dissolve gold to separate it from rock. At Comstock a new process called the Washoe pan process used steam, quicksilver, copper sulfate, and other chemicals. Hard-rock mining had come of age at the Comstock mines.

*Blasting the mountainside with water*

## HYDRAULICKING

In California, industrial mining began with a process called hydraulicking. Powerful water hoses were turned on the cement-like gravel hills to pound them into loose gravel. By 1853, small mining companies employed gangs of miners who used hoses instead of pickaxes. The hoses had nozzles to increase the force of the water shooting out. This pressurized water brought down entire hillsides of gold-bearing gravels. These landslides were then washed through sluices to separate out the gold.

# Dangers of Mining

**G**old seekers who survived the dangers of traveling west faced other hazards in the gold fields. At the diggings, miners lived in tents and shacks. Filth and poor living conditions brought disease. Rats scurried through miners' shanties and over their bedrolls as they slept. In California's wet marshy gold fields, miners became ill with dysentery, typhoid fever, and malaria. Miners themselves called these diseases "Sacramento fever."

In 1850, a cholera epidemic swept through Sacramento and San Francisco. One out of ten Sacramento miners died from this disease. In 1851, one out of 25 miners in Sacramento died of illness. Many others died from other dangers such as floods and fires.

*The Bettmann Archive*

*Prospectors braving a storm*

In 1850, the Sacramento lowlands were flooded by heavy rains and melting mountain snows. Miners in their shacks were swept away and drowned or smothered in deep mud. From 1849 to 1851, San Francisco was hit by many large fires that destroyed whole sections of the growing city. After each tragic blaze, miners buried their dead and rebuilt the town.

Many placer miners panning for gold knee-deep in icy cold streams caught pneumonia and suffered from pain and stiffness. But the worst mining hazards were in the hard-rock mines of Comstock. Nevada's "fifty-niners" tunneled deep underground and dug out underground caverns 100 feet tall. Because this silver-bearing rock crumbled easily, cave-ins were common in the early days at Comstock.

Miners digging loose stone from cavern walls sometimes hit underground hot springs and were scalded by 170-degree water. As the mine tunnels grew longer, the temperature inside them heated up. The temperature rose three degrees every hundred feet of tunnel.

In the Crown Point mine, temperatures got up to 150 degrees. Mining companies had to give miners ice to cool their bodies and tools. A miner could use 95 pounds of ice in a single day.

In 1869, fire struck deep in three Comstock mines when the miners' candles ignited the natural gas underground. Firefighters tried pouring water down the shafts, but cool air rushed down with the water and fanned the flames. Nothing could be done to save the 45 miners trapped below. After five days, the mines were sealed in order to smother the underground blaze. When the tunnels were reopened 14 days later, fresh currents of air again fanned the flames. Three years later, stone walls still glowed red-hot in the reopened mine.

*Fires in mines were common*

Some of the mines went down as deep as 3,000 feet. At that depth, the air was very thin. Miners had difficulty breathing and were often overcome with cramps or "stomach knots." Miners worked in teams. One group rested near the ventilation shaft as the others continued digging. In the deepest mines, men had to rest after just 15 minutes of work.

Deaths and injuries from accidents were common. In 1863, part of the Comstock's Mexican mine collapsed, crushing and smothering miners below. From 1863 to 1880, there were 295 deaths and 608 injuries from mining accidents at Comstock.

Miners were sometimes maimed or killed by heavy machinery. In 1879, a Comstock miner named James Galloway got his sleeve caught in an air blower and died trying to free himself. He'd been a miner for 26 years.

Over time, better mining methods were created. Better blowers improved ventilation, and pumps removed underground water. Mechanical drills made the work easier, and underground wooden frames prevented cave-ins. But while these improvements made mining safer, deep hard-rock mining remained a dangerous line of work.

The Bettmann Archive

*Descending the mine shaft*

# Gold and Silver Rushes

California's Gold Rush was the first, but it wasn't the last. As gold seekers mobbed the diggings, some men felt crowded. Prospectors on the western slopes of the Sierra Nevadas began drifting north and east in search of new diggings. They found what they were looking for.

*Miners on the move—again*

Silver was discovered on the eastern slopes of the Sierras in Nevada. In 1859, a new rush headed for this Washoe region, later called Comstock. During 1860, about 10,000 California prospectors poured over the mountains to Nevada.

A new boom town named Virginia City began to be settled high on Mount Davidson. Miners worked the hard-rock Comstock mines for $4 a day in wages. Between 1860 and 1880, $300 million in gold and silver was mined at Comstock.

*Leadville, Colorado, in the 1870s*

In 1859, "Pike's Peak or Bust" became the slogan of prospectors headed for Colorado. But Colorado's miners didn't come from California. They mostly came from the frontier states of Missouri, Ohio, Indiana, and Illinois. Some 100,000 "fifty-niners" entered Colorado's Rocky Mountains looking for gold. They staked their claims along creeks and valleys north of Denver.

Central City, Colorado, became a boom town during the 1860s. But little gold was found in those first years, and many miners returned home disappointed. A few years later, Central City experienced a second boom.

Colorado's big mining boom came in the late 1870s. Colorado gold panners had been annoyed by the heavy gravels that mixed with their gold. In 1877, these gravels proved to be rich in silver and lead.

*Western gold and silver strike sites*

The town of Leadville soon became the world's largest source of silver. It grew from a small village of 200 people in 1877 to a bustling city of 15,000 in just three years. One hundred new miners entered Leadville each day.

Some of the disappointed Colorado gold seekers headed north to new diggings in Idaho and Montana. In 1864, two prospectors washed gold from gravel deposits in Montana's Silver Bow Creek. News spread. By 1867, 400 prospectors were panning for gold along the creek.

Then, in 1874, a prospector named William Farlin mined black rock rich in silver. Farlin and others staked claims near Butte, Montana. Before long, others discovered they could extract copper from the Butte ore. By 1884, Montana's Anaconda mine near Butte was one of the world's biggest sources of copper.

In the early 1860s, prospectors found gold in the Boise Basin in southwestern Idaho. Gold miners rushed in from California, Colorado, and the Missouri frontier. More than 16,000 gold seekers worked claims in the Boise area in 1864. The gold towns of Placerville, Centerville, and Idaho City boomed with people and trade.

Some prospectors entered Idaho from the Northwest. They had gone north out of California to Washington, Oregon, and British Columbia, a province of Canada. In 1858, 30,000 prospectors headed for the Fraser River region in British Columbia after they heard reports of gold. Miners headed for Wyoming in 1868 and South Dakota and Arizona in the 1870s. The slightest rumor of gold could start a rush.

### ROUGHING IT

In his book *Roughing It*, the famous American writer Mark Twain wrote that he was "smitten with silver fever" as California prospectors rushed to new diggings in Nevada. "In 1858, silver lodes were discovered in Carson County. . . . Prospecting parties were leaving for the mountains every day, and discovering and taking possession of rich silver-bearing loads and ledges of quartz. Plainly this was the road to fortune."

The Bettmann Archive

*A wagon train squeezes through a narrow pass*

# Mining Towns

**S**an Francisco, Virginia City, Denver, and Central City were just a few of the boom towns on the western mining frontier. Gold and silver strikes drew steams of prospectors, business people, gamblers, and thieves. San Francisco, California's "Queen City," was the first.

San Francisco grew from a town with fewer than a thousand people in 1848 to a city of 25,000 one year later. By 1852, 36,000 people, including merchants, bankers, and hotel owners, lived there. The most successful people in the city weren't mud-soaked, gold-crazed miners. They were shopkeepers and suppliers, builders and shippers, realtors and saloon keepers.

San Francisco became the biggest business center in the entire Far West. Manufactured goods and raw materials were shipped from back East to San Francisco's wharfs. Food, clothing, and mining equipment were then loaded onto river steamboats headed to the mining districts. On the way back, these steamers transported forty-niners from the mining camps to the city to spend their gold.

*Helena, Montana, in 1865*

## THE WILD TOWN OF DEADWOOD

In 1876, gold was found near Deadwood Gulch, South Dakota. Within a year, 25,000 people rushed to Deadwood to work quartz mines and build businesses. Deadwood's wealth attracted the famous gunfighter, Wild Bill Hickok. On August 2, 1876, while playing cards, Wild Bill was shot in the back of the head by "Crooked Nose" Jack McCall. Hickok's poker hand—black aces and eights—came to be called "the deadman's hand."

*Miners at Deadwood, 1876*

The Bettmann Archive

In San Francisco's boom days, people walked the streets with gold dust in their pockets. In 1848, at a camp called Dry Diggings, early prospectors panned several ounces—and sometimes even several pounds—of gold in a day. Food and supplies were very expensive, but miners had money for fun as well. Plenty of businesses sprang up to offer it to them. San Francisco's hotels, dance halls, gaming parlors, and saloons kept miners' gold flowing from their pockets.

*Raising a ruckus at the saloon*

After 1859, gold rushes to Nevada, Colorado, and other western mining regions created other boom towns. High on Nevada's Mount Davidson, Virginia City became a busy trade center for the famous Comstock mines. In 1860, some 10,000 California prospectors poured over the Sierra Nevadas to the silver mines of Comstock.

Virginia City had its share of dance halls and saloons, like the popular Walter's Music Hall. However, wealthy Virginia City ladies preferred Piper's Opera House, where they could see Shakespeare's *Hamlet* and hear violin concertos. Meanwhile, the hard-rock miners spent their wages at dog races, bear fights, and wild dance halls known as "hurdy-gurdy" houses.

Denver became the mining hub of Colorado in the early 1860s. As gold strikes were made in the Rocky Mountains, the sleepy foothill town on the plains became a trade center. After the railroad came through in 1870, Denver grew to become a center of commerce for the whole region.

Stagecoaches ran from Denver to nearby Central City and other mountain mining towns. Central City itself became a cultural center, with an opera house and the largest hotel in the state, the four-story Teller House. In 1873, when President Ulysses S. Grant visited Central City, the hotel entrance was paved with solid silver bricks in his honor.

# Law and Disorder

In early boom towns and mining camps, disorder was the rule. Gold seekers just set up tents or shacks and started digging. In 1849, the Far West had been a part of U.S. territory for only a few years. In the mountain wilds of Nevada and Colorado, there was no government at all. Far from the U.S. government in Washington, D.C., miners didn't give much thought to following the law.

Most of the mining lands were owned by the government. The law said that anyone could stake a claim and own the gold that he dug up. Honest prospectors got into fights over claim boundaries. Dishonest miners stole gold from others' claims. This was called claim "jumping." Soon, miners began to see the need for some sort of law and order.

The miners got together and organized mining districts. Each district was governed by an elected mayor called an alcalde. This alcalde system was borrowed from California's old Mexican government. Each town mayor kept a record of claims and their owners. When disagreements arose, they were settled by the alcalde or a panel of miners.

The miners also wrote codes of law to govern mining claims. Early laws ruled that prospectors could own and work only one claim at a time. A miner had to work his claim one out of every three days. If he didn't, someone else could claim it. Unfairly, these town laws didn't protect Mexican, Chilean, and Chinese miners. Other miners could steal their claims without being punished.

*Miners often settled arguments with violence*

The Bettmann Archive

Despite these laws, stealing, violence, and murder occurred often in the gold fields. Miners kept order by capturing accused thieves and forcing them to stand trial. Mayors sometimes acted as judges. Other times, juries of miners were formed to decide a person's innocence or guilt. But miners knew little about how to conduct fair trials. Most people accused of crimes were convicted, though many were probably innocent.

## "HANGTOWN"

In 1848, three prospectors staked a claim at a dry creek near Coloma, California. The camp was called Dry Diggings, then Old Dry Diggings, and finally Ravine City. In 1849, a gang of Ravine City thieves received 39 lashes for attempted robbery. After the whippings, three of the thieves were accused of other crimes. They were promptly hanged and left to swing from an oak tree. The town was renamed "Hangtown." Then in 1851, Hangtown changed its name again, to Placerville.

*Punishment was harsh on the mining frontier*

Since there were no jails, punishment came in the form of fines paid in gold, whipping, maiming, branding, or hanging. At a Sierra camp called Dry Town, a miner named George Gillin received 39 lashes for stealing another miner's gold. At Shasta City, a miner who killed his partner was quickly tried and hanged.

Angry miners sometimes formed vigilante groups and punished accused men without giving them a trial. At the Oregon Bar camp, a miner named Walden was strung up by the neck to make him confess to stealing. He was tortured this way several times, but he pleaded that he was innocent. The disappointed miners finally let him go. In San Francisco, the criminal Samuel Whittaker was kidnapped from his jail cell and lynched by a mob.

Vigilantes sometimes hanged the wrong man. In Vaca Valley in 1857, vigilantes lynched a Mexican miner for horse thieving. Later, he was found to be innocent. Such was the rule of law in western mining camps.

*A vigilante lassos his prey*

25

# Indians on the Mining Frontier

The Aztecs of Mexico and the Incas of Peru made gold jewelry and other objects long before Columbus arrived in 1492. In California the Indians knew of gold deposits in the Sierras. But they liked turquoise stone better. The Spanish invaders, however, were wild about gold. After stealing all the gold of the Aztecs and Incas, the conquistadors rode north to find more.

In 1540, Coronado entered the Southwest in search of the fabled Seven Cities of Cibola, said to be rich in gold. Earlier explorers had reported seeing these golden cities in present-day New Mexico. But instead of gold, Coronado found mud-walled adobe pueblos, or towns, of the Zuñi Indians. In bright sunlight, the adobe dwellings appeared to shine like gold.

Later, the Spanish claimed the southwest of North America and told the Indians that they had to obey them. Spanish missions were built to convert Native Americans to Christianity. Indians were forced to work in Spanish mines. In 1680, the Pueblo Indians rose up against the Spanish and forced them back to old Mexico.

But the flow of white men into Native American lands could not be stopped. By the time gold was discovered in 1848, the U.S. had taken California and the Southwest from Mexico in the Mexican-American War.

When gold was struck on John Sutter's property in California in 1848, Sutter arranged with the Coloma Indians for a lease on their lands in the Sierra foothills. That was the last time anyone asked the California Indians for permission to mine their homelands. Miners swarmed over Indian lands. They carved up the mountains, muddied the streams, and scared away game animals.

The Indians' traditional way of life was destroyed. When they resisted, they were attacked. Entire Indian villages in the Sierra foothills were destroyed. Native

*California and the Southwest were part of Mexico before 1848*

The Bettmann Archive

*The discovery of gold in California*

26

people were murdered or driven away. Some California Indians became miners and worked for very low wages in labor gangs. But as more forty-niners arrived in the gold fields, these Indians were driven off too.

*An Indian pueblo*

In the Southwest, Apache and Navajo warriors were successful for a while in keeping miners off their native lands. Gold was found in 1860 at Pinos Altos in New Mexico. Miners rushed in from California, Mexico, and Texas, only to be driven out by the Apaches. Apaches also kept miners away from the gold and silver strikes in Arizona until the 1870s.

In Montana and Idaho, miners tried to push their way into Indian lands. But the local Indians kept them out for many years.

After the Civil War, however, the U.S. Army was sent west to drive the Indians from their lands. The government wanted to open up the West for ranching, homesteading, and mining. After much bloodshed, western mining regions were opened to prospecting. And the highly valued gold and silver was freely taken from Indian homelands.

Few Indians survived the army's attacks and the diseases brought by white men. Most of those who did were forced onto reservations throughout the West.

## BLACK HILLS OF GOLD

In 1868, the government signed a treaty promising that miners would stay out of the Sioux's sacred Black Hills in South Dakota. But in 1876, the government went back on its word and opened the Black Hills to mining. The Sioux were very angry and began attacking mining camps. On June 25, 1876, General George Custer and his army were defeated in the Battle of the Little Bighorn as they tried to wipe out the Sioux.

*General George Custer*

# Mule Trains and Muleteers

Forty-niners lived in isolated mountain mining camps and boom towns. These growing settlements needed a steady supply of clothing, food, tools, medicines, liquors, and even bar mirrors and pianos. The goods were shipped to San Francisco ports on boats from back East. Supplies were then loaded onto steamboats and taken up rivers to towns like Sacramento.

From there, supplies were packed onto wagons for the trip over land to the mining towns. But once they reached the mountains, wagons could not travel over steep mountain trails.

Before the Gold Rush, many Mexican pioneers had learned to walk long strings of mules over narrow, difficult trails. The people who did this were called *arrieros*, or "muleteers." The long line of mules were called "mule trains." The mules were tied together and walked nose to tail. They were loaded with heavy packs filled with supplies of all sorts. Packing the mules and driving a mule train took great skill.

Muleteers cushioned the mules' backs with thick pads and spoke calmly to the animals to reassure them while packing. They even blindfolded mules during loading to keep them from bucking and pitching. The mules' heavy loads had to be balanced very carefully.

*A mule train*

The lead mule in the train was a white or gray female, called a mare, with a bell tied around her neck. Pack mules were trained to follow this "bell mare" by sight and sound.

Mule trains moved slowly, but steadily. By 1855, some 30,000 mules were carrying supplies into isolated mining towns in California. Many mule trains included over 150 mules.

The muleteers' day started early with a breakfast of beans and tortillas or corn bread. Then the work of loading and packing the mules began. After a long morning climbing

*Mules were blindfolded during loading*

through the hills, the train stopped for a lunch break and watering. The drive then continued until day's end when the train was stopped for the night. Packs and pads were removed, and the mules were turned loose to eat wild grasses.

*Tramping through a snowy pass*

Muleteers suppered on beef jerky and more tortillas and beans. Then they bedded down to sleep. Through the night, guards called night riders kept a watch on the mule herd in shifts. The next morning, the last shift of night riders rounded up the mules for packing.

After 1858, gold districts of the Far West spread past California's borders. There were gold rushes to the Northwest and gold and silver rushes to Nevada and Colorado. Wherever prospectors dug in, there was a need for supplies.

Pack-mule trains carried supplies from ports on the Columbia River to diggings in Montana, and from the west coast to the mining districts of eastern Oregon. Mule trains also carried mail to the mines as well as gold from the mines for shipment to banks.

In later years, the trails to the mines were widened into roads that wagons could use. But on the steepest, narrowest trails, nothing but mule trains could get through.

## MULE-SKINNERS AND WAGONS

On good mountain roads, freight wagons could carry supplies to the mines. Teams of six to eight mules were hitched to supply wagons driven by "mule-skinners." Freight wagons also carried supplies across the Great Plains to mining camps in Colorado. Some of these wagons were pulled by teams of oxen instead of mules. In 1858, one large company used 3,500 wagons, 40,000 oxen, and 1,000 mules.

29

# Songs of the Forty-Niners

On the overland trails, on ships, and in the jungles of Panama, gold seekers entertained themselves with songs as they headed for the diggings. They sang of high hopes and the dangers of travel. They often made up new words to old tunes like the popular song "Oh! Susanna."

*Oh I came from Salem City with my washbowl on my knee,*
*I'm going to California, the gold dust for to see.*
*It rained all night, the day I left, the weather it was dry,*
*The sun so hot I froze to death, oh, brothers don't you cry!*

*Oh! California, that's the land for me,*
*I'm going to Sacramento, with my washbowl on my knee.*

One of the favorite songs of miners who traveled to California across the Great Plains was "Sweet Betsy From Pike." Betsy and Ike set out from Missouri. Along the west-bound trail, their cattle die, their food gives out, and Betsy gets sick.

*Oh, don't you remember*
  *sweet Betsy from Pike,*
*Who crossed the big moun-*
  *tains with her lover Ike,*
*With two yoke of cattle,*
  *a large yellow dog,*
*A tall Shanghai rooster and*
  *one spotted hog.*

*Betsy collapses in the heat*

*They soon reached the desert, where Betsy gave out,*
*And down in the sand she lay rolling about,*
*While Ike, half-distracted, looked on with surprise,*
*Saying, "Betsy, get up, you'll get sand in your eyes."*

Most forty-niners left their family and friends behind to try their luck on the mining frontier. But when they reached the diggings, many found the "pickin's" slim—too many miners and not enough gold. So they moved on to the next camp— and the next—like the homeless miner in this song:

30

## OH, MY DARLIN'!

In gold towns like San Francisco, the forty-niners' home-spun ballads found their way into music halls and theaters. The sad song "Clementine" was a mining camp and dance hall favorite.

*In a cavern, in a canyon, excavating for a mine,*
*Lived a miner, forty-niner and his daughter Clementine.*
*Oh, my darlin', oh, my darlin', oh, my darlin' Clementine,*
*You are lost and gone forever, dreadful sorry, Clementine.*

*Miners' tunes became dance hall favorites*

*When I got there, the mining ground*
*Was staked and claimed for miles around,*
*And not a bed was to be found, when I went off to prospect.*
*The town was crowded full of folks,*
*Which made me think 'twas not a hoax,*
*At my expense they cracked their jokes, when I was nearly starving.*

The miners sang of broken hearts and broken bones, bad habits, hard luck, and gold strikes. One song followed a "greenhorn," or newcomer, from the Missouri across the plains and mountains to California.

*I've just got in across the Plains,*
*    I'm poorer than a snail,*
*My mules all died, but poor old Clip,*
*    I pulled in by the tail.*
*I fed him last at Chimney Rock,*
*    that's where the grass gave out,*
*I'm proud to tell, we stood it well,*
*    along the Truckee route.*

*A coffee break*

Miners depended on good luck and good humor for survival. That's why their songs poked fun at hard times and talked about hope for better days.

# In the Miners' Own Words

In letters back home and to newspapers, miners wrote about life in the diggings. Some of them started diaries along the trails or on board ship. Some told the truth, but others stretched it a little—and sometimes even told outright lies. Here's part of a letter from a son to his mother, written while he crossed the western plains:

*August 25, 1850*
*Dear Mother,*
*I take this opportunity to let you know how we are getting along. . . . We have had no trouble on the road yet and are getting along very well with our journey. . . . Our horses stand the trip as well as can be expected. There are many fresh graves that we have seen on the road. If you can find any way to send me a letter to Sacramento City, if I get there, I will be apt to get it.*
*Your Obedient Son,*
*S.E. Hardy*

*Miners were eager to hear news from home*

Crossing the plains to California was dangerous. Gold seekers suffered hunger, thirst, disease, and Indian attacks. A traveler named Lemuel Clarke McKeeby wrote this in his diary while crossing the Humbolt River trail in Nevada:

*July 13, 1850*
*Tonight we eat the last of our provisions. We are not alone in our trouble in this respect. There are thousands who have been running out of grub for the past week. I never saw such hungry men. Many talk seriously of killing their horses and eating them and running the risk of getting through on foot. . . . The road is lined with the carcasses of dead horses and cattle. The stench from them as we pass is horrid and sickening.*

Gold seekers sacrificed their lives, farms, and savings to get to California. When they finally arrived—if they arrived—they wanted to report good news. *The New York Herald* newspaper published this letter from the diggings. It's probably not a true story.

*August 15, 1848*
*Mr. Editor,*
*I have now spent several*
*months at the gold "placero".... I*
*find these dry diggings far exceed*
*anything that has been discovered.*
*The pieces found here are of an*
*astonishing size. The largest piece ...*
*weighs about thirteen pounds....*
*Instances have occurred here where men*
*have carried the earth on their backs and*
*collected $800 to $1500 a day....*
*Yours, Fortunately,*
*J.B.*

*Reading letters from distant loved ones*

Letters sent back East, truthful or not, attracted even more gold seekers. Many traveled on riverboats to Missouri, where the trails started west. But riverboat travel was dangerous, too. A man named Robert Chalmers made these entries in his diary:

*April 23, 1850*
*About midnight, the captain came down and gave the alarm that the boat was on fire.... I got together what clothes I could and put out. By this time, the fire was rushing forward rapidly.*

*May 3, 1850*
*Another man fell overboard and drowned. He was a young Irishman and a smart young fellow. But the river runs rapid and water whirls and the banks are steep. If a man gets in, it is impossible to get him out.*

## BUFFALO THUNDER

On the trails west, gold seekers saw buffalo for the first time. On May 29, 1850, Lemuel McKeeby wrote this in his diary:

*A drove of buffalo came charging towards the river. They came on like an avalanche with noise like thunder.... Thousands in number ... they dashed through the river without a halt ... stampeding the horses and doing damage.*

# Tall Tales of the Gold Rush

Forty-niners joined the Gold Rush with high hopes. They were encouraged by fantastic reports of huge gold strikes in California. Stories of 25-pound gold nuggets were common.

Most miners, however, were lucky to pan a few ounces of gold a day. A prospector worked day after day hoping to strike it rich. Stories of gold strikes sent him packing to the next gold field, or the next mountain, or the next state. A lot of these reports started when prospectors told stories for entertainment after a hard day's work.

One popular old story was told about a gold strike in a cemetery. It went something like this:

*Prospectors sometimes exaggerated their gold findings. Here, miners weigh their gold dust.*

UPI/Bettmann

*Back in the first days of the Rush, you could find gold just about anywhere. I had a partner on Rich Ravine who died of a fever. So we hauled his body over to the cemetery for proper burial. Well, we dug us a grave with our pickaxes and shovels and piled the earth and gravels right next to it. Then we lowered Old Todd's coffin down into it and one of the boys started reading from a Bible. The prayers sounded pretty good and a few of us were wet-eyed. I shed a tear or two myself, thinking about my unfortunate friend. But just as we were listening to the Lord's Prayer, one old miner cried out, "Hold it right there! We've struck gold, boys!" And he was right! Sitting there in that pile of grave dirt was a shining gold nugget! We hauled poor Todd's coffin back out and set to digging.*

PRACTICAL JOKES

Miners often played jokes on "greenhorns." That's what they called miners new to the diggings. Sometimes a prospector would load gold flakes like buckshot into a shotgun and fire it into the ground. He'd then spread the word that he'd found a new strike. More than one newspaper reporter was tricked this way. One forty-niner fired gold into several trees. He then tricked a greenhorn into believing that gold grew on the glittering trees.

*Playing a joke on a greenhorn*

Prospectors depended on their burros or donkeys for carrying tools and supplies to and from the diggings. Colorado miners affectionately called their donkeys "Rocky Mountain canaries." One favorite story told of a prospector who prided himself on his burro's intelligence and "gold-sense." It went like this:

*I was prospecting out of Breckenridge in '59, when my burro run off. That wasn't the first time she did that. She'd done it on the South Platte and over near Fairplay six months before. Both times I spent better part of a day rounding her up. And I lost valuable digging time doing it. So this time I was mad and fit to be tied myself. She was a smart old gal and I depended on her—so I went off to locate her. I trailed her up a ravine to a dry creek bed. And there she was kicking at the gravel and braying something awful. Looked like she'd gotten a fever and was about to throw fits! I ran up angry and grabbed her bridle. And then I saw them, right there at her feet—gold nuggets. My old gal had wandered off in search of gold! She must've gotten a whiff of gold on the air. Who can say? But that old burro had a "gold-sense" better than any man. That was the biggest strike I ever made.*

*A burro with "gold sense"*

# Bonanza Kings and Paupers

Not every prospector with a pickax struck it rich. Most of the hardest-working miners died poor and forgotten.

John Sutter was an immigrant from Switzerland who arrived in California around 1839. He created a huge, successful ranch in the Sacramento Valley. There, he raised wheat, planted fruit trees, and built a fort, a tannery, and a flour mill. In 1847, a carpenter named John Marshall discovered gold at Sutter's sawmill. It was the beginning of the end for them both.

The gold rush to California rushed right over them. Thousands of forty-niners invaded Sutter's lands looking for gold. They trampled his wheat, scattered his cattle, and tore apart his buildings for wood planking. He tried to fight for his rights in court but lost.

Finally, Sutter left California and moved east. He died broke in a Washington, D.C., hotel room in 1880. The only gold he had was a ring made from the first gold found at his mill.

John Marshall staked a claim near Sutter's mill. But gold seekers overran his property too and built a mining town right on top of it. He left the area to prospect elsewhere. But wherever he went, others followed. They thought he had a magic touch for finding gold. As soon as he made a strike, hordes of other prospectors crowded in on top of his claim. He died penniless in 1885.

*Only a few prospectors ever found nuggets as large as these*

UPI/Bettmann

## BANKING ON SILVER

Mining made William C. Ralston of San Francisco a wealthy man—but he never swung a pickax. Instead, he opened a bank called the Bank of California. A tough and clever businessman, he soon owned all of the stamp mills at Comstock. Eventually, he also owned mines, mills, and railroads. In 1875, Ralston's bank went bankrupt. He was found floating dead in San Francisco Bay.

In the first year of the California rush, a prospector could make quite a bit of money. But few of them became rich. In just a few years, most of the gold that was lying loose in streams and sand bars had been found. To make a lot of money, a miner then had to dig into the rocky mountainside to uncover veins of gold.

This is when mining became big business and took a lot of equipment and money to operate. Most prospectors finally had to go to work for the big mines. They were never paid very much for their labor.

*John Marshall was followed wherever he went*

The hard-rock mines in the Comstock area, however, made a few businessmen very rich. Large sums of money were needed to operate these mines. So groups of businessmen put their money together to build and operate a mine. If the mine made lots of money, the men who owned it became rich. These men became known as "bonanza kings."

Irish-born John Mackay was a forty-niner during the Gold Rush. In the 1860s, he and three other Irish miners—James Fair, James Flood, and William O'Brien—became supervisors in the Comstock mines. Together, the Irishmen bought into several mines.

The partners got lucky. Their Consolidated Virginia mine struck rich pay dirt that came to be called the Big Bonanza. Mackay and his partners became rich beyond their wildest dreams. Between 1873 and 1882, the Big Bonanza produced more than a hundred million dollars in silver.

*A group of successful prospectors*

# Ghost Towns

Some mining towns, like Denver and San Francisco, grew to be major American cities. Other boom towns, like Central City, Colorado, and Tombstone, Arizona, became tourist centers after the mines closed. But others, like Gila City, Arizona, and Bullfrog, Nevada, were deserted when the mines gave out.

Long toms, sluices, shacks, and saloons were all left behind to collect dust and tumbleweeds. People said that only ghosts continued to live in the deserted towns. The town of Washington on California's Yuba River was a ghost town as early as 1850. In California's Mother Lode region, dozens of other ghost towns still cling to the hills.

*Wolves are the only residents of this ghost town*

The Bettmann Archive

Where hydraulicking was used, powerful water hoses tore down hills and houses that stood in the way. Water hoses swept away half of the town of Volcano, California. In its heyday, Volcano had 47 saloons, 12 restaurants, and the three-story St. George Hotel. What's left of Volcano still stands today— some old stone buildings and tumbled-down houses.

In another California ghost town, Rough and Ready, only one or two buildings are still standing. But in 1851, it was a busy mining town with 6,000 citizens. Angry over federal mining laws, the townspeople voted to secede from the U.S. and form their own independent country.

In 1850, the country of Rough and Ready had its own president and secretary of state. But after just a few months, the citizens voted to rejoin the United States. By 1859, gold deposits gave out and a fire swept through the town. Miners packed up and headed for other diggings.

Bodie, California, was a successful mining town in the 1860s and 1870s. A vein of gold lay under the town, two and a half miles long and almost a mile wide. By 1877, Bodie had 15,000 people, three breweries, three newspapers, and two cemeteries.

The Bettmann Archive

*Eureka, Colorado*

Bodie was nicknamed "Shooting Town." During just one week in 1879, six men were shot to death on the town's streets. By 1883, most of the gold in the mines was used up. By 1946, only eight people still lived in the once-booming Bodie. All that remains today are a few abandoned buildings. Haunted winds blow through Bodie's old cemeteries.

Another haunted cemetery is Tombstone's Boot Hill in the Arizona desert. In 1878, silver was discovered at Tombstone's Lucky Cuss and Tough Nut mines. More than 20,000 people rushed to Tombstone to mine silver, gamble, and raise a ruckus. The town's reputation for lawlessness, fighting, and claim jumping was well known.

One of the most famous shoot-outs in the Old West occurred at Tombstone's O.K. Corral in 1881. The Earp brothers and Doc Holliday killed three outlaws in a spray of thirty bullets. Tombstone's mines gave out by 1890 and its people moved on. Today, Boot Hill is a tourist attraction. On one old tombstone are the words:

*Here lies Lester Moore,*
*Four slugs from a .44,*
*No Less, No more.*

*Boot Hill in Tombstone, Arizona*

## GOLDFIELD, NEVADA

A Shoshone Indian named Tom Fisherman was the first to find gold in this part of Nevada. But the rush didn't hit until 1903 when two other prospectors located a rich lode. Mining companies dug tunnels and paid miners $3.50 a day to haul out gold-bearing rock. In 1910, some 30,000 people lived in Goldfield. But by 1918 all the gold had been taken out and the mines closed. Today, Goldfield's stone buildings stand empty.

# Mining and the Environment

**G**old rushes in the Sierras, Rockies, and throughout the West left scars on the American landscape. Prospectors cared little about the ecology of the regions they mined. As far as the gold seekers were concerned, the mining frontier was broad, wild, and there for the taking.

In the 1800s, many Americans believed that God meant for the U.S. to own all of the land from the east coast to the west coast. Settlers pushed west past the Mississippi River to Oregon. The Southwest and California were taken from Mexico in the Mexican-American War. Texas cattle ranchers drove huge herds of cows across Indian lands to Kansas and further north. To feed the workers who built the railroads, most of the wild buffalo were killed.

*Mining leaves piles of waste, called tailings*

The discovery of gold in California brought swarms of people from the East and other parts of the world to the western United States. The government said that anyone who found gold or other minerals in the West could claim them.

Mining requires digging up the land. Ore deposits were found mixed with gravels and sands or trapped in rocky mountainsides. Miners dug through this rock in a frenzy, searching for its hidden treasures.

*Strip mining scars the land*

Gold dredges were huge floating machines designed to work stream beds. They inched along, churning up gravel and boulders from stream bottoms. An early version of the gold dredge was used on California's Feather River, but it wasn't effective. Later versions proved better at sifting gold-bearing gravels in creek beds. But the gold dredge left a mess of overturned gravel and stone in its path, burying fertile soils deep below.

First with knives and spoons, then with pickaxes and shovels, they dug and sifted the ore deposits. They worked their way up mountain faces, removing bigger and bigger chunks of stone. They blasted the hillsides with dynamite. They stamped and crushed rock to extract gold and used chemicals to dissolve it out of rock. Wherever miners worked, they left scars on the landscape and dirty piles of debris.

Whole mountainsides were ground down by water forced through hoses in hydraulic mining. These powerful jets of water cut through hillsides and brought down trees and stones in avalanches. On the hills and streams below, placer miners were flooded out. California valleys like the Bear River and Steep Hollow were buried under hundreds of feet of sand, stone, and gravel.

Farmlands in the lower valleys were flooded with mining waters that carried mining waste. Silt, or fine sands, clogged rivers and prevented the passage of boats. Waters were muddied all the way to San Francisco Bay. Streams once filled with salmon were poisoned. America's first ecologists, the Indians, saw their ancestral lands and food sources destroyed.

Forests of oak and pine in California were cut down to make cabins, sluices, and dams. Miles and miles of Sierra trees were cut down for use inside the

*Wild animals fled the mining areas*

Comstock mines or to burn in their boilers. More than 80 miles of wooden troughs were built to carry logs down mountainsides and through canyons to Virginia City mines.

Wild animals fled or died as the rivers and forests where they lived were polluted or destroyed. In mining regions, the American wilderness was permanently harmed. The scars can still be seen today in the old mining frontiers of the West.

# Prospecting Today

Though California's Gold Rush ended more than a hundred years ago, prospecting is still possible today. The old-timers didn't scrape every ounce of gold from the mountains. They missed some. And over the years, erosion has continued. Melting snow and mountain floods still occur in the Sierras and Rockies. Water still washes over ancient deposits, exposing gold and sweeping it to the bottom of stream beds.

On public lands in 32 states, gold claims can still be staked. Most of the deposits are in the western states of California, Colorado, Nevada, South Dakota, and Alaska. Just like in the old days, the trick is finding the gold and getting it out of the ground.

The forty-niners used to say, "Gold is where you find it." They were right. But if you know where to look for gold, your chances of finding it are better.

Early prospectors found gold in placer deposits in the foothills. These placer gravels and sands had eroded from veins or lodes in mountain bedrock. Gold-bearing gravels were carried down mountain slopes and deposited in stream beds, crevices, and sand bars.

*This prospector, nicknamed "Daddy," sought gold in British Columbia*

The Bettmann Archive

Today's prospectors find gold in placers just like the forty-niners did. But if you go prospecting, don't expect to strike it rich. Fewer than one in a thousand old-time prospectors ever made a strike. But prospecting as a hobby can be fun and rewarding. Using the tools and methods of the forty-niners, you can still find nuggets and small gold particles, called "colors."

The basic tools for working placer deposits are a shovel, a gold pan, and a pickax. Other useful tools are a magnifying glass, a bucket, and tweezers. To find your way to the diggings, you'll need a topographical map of the area you want to prospect. A topographical map shows hills and valleys and how steep they are. These maps are available from the U.S. Geological Survey, at camping stores, and ranger stations.

*Prospecting tools*

It's best to do some research on the area you plan to prospect. The U.S. Geological Survey lists more than 500 known gold districts. These are good places to start looking. For safety's sake, it's wise to prospect with a partner. Bring food, water, and a first aid kit. And before setting out, let the local Forest Service know your route.

To find deposits, learn to "read" both wet and dry stream beds. Placer gold gets trapped in cracks and crevices, behind boulders and tree stumps, and in gravel and sand bars near bends in the stream. Gold is heavy and sinks down to the bottom of cracks and bars, so you'll need to dig down deep.

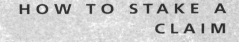

*UPI/Bettmann*

*Prospecting for gold the old-fashioned way*

## HOW TO STAKE A CLAIM

If you find gold on public lands, you must register a formal claim with the government. On a piece of paper write the name of your claim, your name and address, the date, and a description of the area that you are claiming. Place the notice in a tin can and bury it under a three-foot pile of rocks. This pile is called your "discovery monument." You'll also have to record your claim at the local County Recorders Office. The maximum size for an individual claim is 20 acres. Mark the four corners of your claim boundary with other piles of stone.

DISCOVERY MONUMENT

*It's easy to build a discovery monument*

Survey the area you choose to prospect. Take test samples of pay dirt and see how they pan out.

Panning requires patience and good wrist action. Scoop some dirt into the pan, then wash and break up any clumps. You can dip the pan beneath the surface of the water and let the stream carry away lighter materials. Shake and swirl the pan to bring lighter materials to the surface. This will also help settle heavier particles to the pan bottom. Black metallic sands will also settle to the bottom.

As a last step, swirl this muddy mixture with an eye peeled for gold specks. Remove any gold with tweezers and place it in a container.

Unlike the forty-niner, today's prospector is responsible for leaving the land the way he or she found it. So don't tear up the wilderness—even if you get lucky and strike it rich!

*Alaska miners with their picks and shovels*

# INDEX

alcalde—mayor, from old Mexican form of local government, 24

*arrastra*—type of Mexican mill used to crush stone, 17

Black Hills, S.D.,

Boothill, Ariz., 39

buffalo, 40

Butte, Mont., 21

cattle drives, 40

Central City, Colo., 20, 23

Chinese miners, 8

claim staking, 9, 43

Comstock Lode mine, 9, 17, 19, 20

Coronado, Francisco Vásquez de—Spanish explorer who came to the New World seeking gold, 2, 26

coyoting—method of prospecting in which narrow holes and tunnels were dug through gravel to bedrock to find gold-bearing rock, 14

Custer, Gen. George, 26

Deadwood, S.D., 22

Denver, Colo., 23

diggings, *see* mining camps

disease, 6, 10, 18

donkeys, 35

dredge—floating machine that churns up gravel and rock from stream bottoms, 41

Earp brothers, 39

entertainment, 11, 23

environment, 40-41

ghost towns, 38-39

gold
    discovery of, 3
    "fever," 4-5
    geology of, 12-13
    history of, 2
    routes to, 6-7
    rushes, 20-21

Goldfield, Nev., 39

hard-rock mining (also called quartz mining)—digging in solid rock, on mountainsides or in underground tunnels, for gold, silver, or some other mineral, 16-17

Hickok, Wild Bill, 22

Holliday, Doc, 39

hydraulicking—method of mining in which powerful water hoses are used to pound solid rock into loose gravel, 17, 38, 41

Indians, 26-27

Leadville, Colo., 21

lode (also called a vein)—a mineral deposit between layers of rock, 12

Mackay, John, 37

Marshall, John, 3, 36

Mexico, 2, 3, 27

miners, 4, 5, 8-9
    letters and diaries of, 32-33
    songs of, 30-31
    stories of, 34-35

mining
    camps, 10-11, 18
    dangers of, 18-19
    hard-rock, 16-17
    placer, 14
    quartz, 16-17
    river, 15

muleteer—someone who drives a mule train, 28, 29

mule train, 28, 29

panning—method of prospecting in which gravel from a stream bed is washed in a pan to separate the gold, 14, 44

placer—a deposit of sand or gravel left by moving water that contains mineral particles, 13

placer mining—searching for gold in placer deposits, 14

prospectors, *see* miners

quartz mining, see hard-rock mining

Ralston, William, 36

rocker (also called a cradle)—wooden box on rockers that sifted out worthless rocks and gravel while trapping heavy gold-bearing rock, 15

Rocky Mountains, 20, 21

routes to the gold
overland, 7
Panama, 6
sea, 6

San Francisco, 3, 4, 22

Seven Cities of Cibola—fabled cities of gold that Coronado searched for in 1540, 26

Sierra Nevada mountains, 10, 13, 16, 20

silver, 12, 20

sluice (also called a sluice box)—several toms placed end to end, used for prospecting, 15

songs, 30-31

Spaniards, 2, 26

stamp mill—type of mill that stamps on rock to free the gold or other mineral embedded in it, 17

Sutter, John, 3, 36

tailings—waste left behind by mining, 41

tom (also called a long tom)—long wooden trough, similar to a rocker, used for prospecting, 15

tools, 14-15, 42

towns
ghost, 38-39
mining, 10, 11, 20, 21, 22-23

Twain, Mark—American writer and novelist (1835–1910), 21

vein (also called a lode)—a long deposit of mineral between layers of rock, 12

vigilantes—angry citizens who took the law into their own hands although they had no legal authority to use force or arrest people, 25

Virginia City, Nev., 20, 23

violence, 24-25, 39

women, 5, 8, 9